Recent revelations that North Korea has maintained its nuclear weapon program in violation of prior international agreements highlight the adversarial relationship between Washington and Pyongyang.[1] For 50 years, American foreign policy has tried to co-opt or shun North Korea, usually without success. Prior U.S. attempts at engagement have been half-hearted at best, often being nothing more than an opportunity for Pyongyang to extract concessions from the West. The United States should re-evaluate its approach toward North Korea and implement a comprehensive and integrated strategy that offers tangible incentives for cooperation backed by substantial costs for non-compliance.

Such a strategy is presented in part one of this paper. U.S. objectives toward North Korea are identified and prioritized; the effectiveness of diplomatic, economic, information, and military means toward North Korea are presented; and a plan for implementing these options is developed. Part two assumes that peaceful options for attaining U.S. goals in North Korea fail and that Washington must resort to military force. Capabilities, constraints, and goals of the antagonists are identified and assumptions made about their likely courses of action. From this framework a military strategy is presented that provides a viable alternative for the United States.

I.

Strategic Objectives

The number one priority for Washington is to ensure that Pyongyang does not develop or acquire the means to unleash the horrors of nuclear war. North Korea, realizing that its power is diminishing relative to its neighbors and the West, has been pursuing nuclear weapons for years.

---

[1] "U.S. Tells N. Korea Disarm or Face Global Pressure," World, CNN.com, 19 October 2002, <http://www.cnn.com/2002/WORLD/asiapcf/east/10/19/nkorea.nukes/index html> (19 October 2002).

Recent U.S. intelligence estimates indicate Pyongyang has accomplished all of the phases of nuclear warhead manufacturing and may have enough fuel to produce one or two weapons.[2] Should Kim Jong-Il develop the capability to use these weapons, Japan and South Korea would be held hostage to Pyongyang's bellicose policies. Perhaps more disturbing is the possibility that North Korea will share these weapons with states or groups hostile to the United States or its allies.

North Korean scientists are also developing ballistic missiles capable of striking targets 4,000 miles away. The Taepo Dong series of intermediate-range missiles is the most sophisticated offensive weapon system outside the major nuclear powers. Once fully operational, the Taepo Dong-II would be capable of striking any country in Asia, as well as Alaska and Hawaii.[3] Moreover, Pyongyang has sold these missiles, or the technology behind them, to nations openly or potentially hostile to the United States.[4] As a second priority, the United States must freeze North Korea's development of intermediate- and long-range missiles and block their transfer to additional rogue states.

The Korean Peninsula remains a fertile ground for conventional warfare. North and South Korea have technically been at war for more than fifty years and two of the most potent land armies in the world face one another across a fragile demilitarized zone (DMZ).[5] The threat of

---

[2] Notra Trulock, "Going Nuclear in North Korea; Regime May Have One or Two Bombs Already." The Washington Times 25 June 2002, OPED, p. A19. LexisNexis Academic (2 October 2002).

[3] Kenneth G. Weiss, "The Limits of Diplomacy: Missile Proliferation, Diplomacy, and Defense," World Affairs, Winter 2001, v. 163-3, pp. 110-122. ProQuest (2 October 2002). Table 1: The Missile Capabilities of Proliferant Countries.

[4] Weiss, "The Limits of Diplomacy: Missile Proliferation, Diplomacy, and Defense."

[5] U.S. Department of Defense, 2000 Report to Congress: Military Situation on the Korean Peninsula, Defense Link, September 2000, <http://www.defenselink mil/news/Sep2000/korea09122000 html> (19 October 2002). Section One: Deterrence and Defense on the Korean Peninsula.

invasion keeps tensions high and diverts attention and resources away from other needs and opportunities. As such, a third priority for the United States is to reduce the conventional military threat on the peninsula in a manner that gives both sides confidence that they will not be attacked.

A divided Korea is a relic of the Cold War and remains an unnatural solution to a political struggle that essentially ended with the demise of the Soviet Union in 1991. In every case since World War II, people within a partitioned country have sought reunification. In Germany, this process was achieved peacefully; in Vietnam, reunification was achieved by force. Because the division of the Korean people is the main and underlying source of tension on the peninsula, the fourth, albeit long-term, priority for the United States is the peaceful reunification of the two Koreas under a democratic government.

Strategic Options

The United States has several means it can employ for achieving its strategic objectives on the Korean Peninsula. First and foremost is diplomacy. Bilateral relations with the North can be difficult given the vast differences between Washington and Pyongyang. Fortunately, the United States has strong Asian allies in Japan and South Korea that have common interests toward North Korea. Together, these three nations can provide a multilateral approach to modifying North Korean behavior. Moreover, North Korea is politically isolated. Barely 20 nations maintain embassies in Pyongyang and old allies, such as the former Soviet Union and China, are becoming friendlier with the United States.[6] Moscow and Beijing are undergoing enormous

---

[6] Doug Bandow, "Rethinking the North Korean Threat." Newsday, 22 August 1999, Cato Institute, <http://www.cato.org/cgi-bin/scripts/printtech.cgi/dailys/08-27-99.html> (8 October 2002).

social, political, and economic changes that, with U.S. assistance, can provide an example for

Pyongyang to move in a more positive direction.[7]

Economically, North Korea is a failed state. South Korea possesses 30 times the GDP and

twice the population of the North.[8] Real economic growth in the North is declining by 3%

annually with no improvement in sight.[9] Although Pyongyang has an abundance of raw

minerals, it is dependent upon imports of oil to keep its meager industry running. On top of this,

alternating droughts and floods have decimated its agricultural sector. North Korea cannot feed

its people and must rely on foreign aid to survive. These factors make economic assistance or

sanctions important options for the United States and its allies. The United States, Japan, and

South Korea possess the first, third, and thirteenth highest GDPs in the world.[10] These countries

can easily offer Pyongyang bilateral and multilateral economic aid packages (or threaten to

withhold them) in return for working toward the four objectives.

Diplomacy and economic aid are supported by military might. The United States has the

most powerful military on earth and while only 37,000 American soldiers are stationed in South

Korea, Washington can quickly deploy thousands more.[11] Technical superiority in firepower

---

[7] Lee Hoi-Chang, "Korea at the Crossroads: The Challenges Ahead." Heritage Lectures, The Heritage Foundation, No. 728, 23 January 2002, <http://www.heritage.org/library/lecture/hl728 html> (7 October 2002).

[8] Doug Bandow, "Hugs for Pyongyang," The Washington Times, 4 October 1999, Cato Institute, <http://www.cato.org/cgi-bin/scripts/printtech.cgi/dailys/10-08-99.html> (8 October 2002).

[9] "Korea, North," World Countries. Infoplease.com. 2002, <http://www.infoplease.com/ipa/A0107686 html> (2 October 2002). Economic Summary.

[10] The World Almanac and Book of Facts 2002, s.v. "Countries With Highest Gross Domestic Product and Per Capita GDP." p. 106.

[11] Bernard E. Trainor, "A Second Korean War?" Marine Corps Gazette, August 1997, v. 81-8, pp. 26-7. ProQuest. (2 October 2002).

combined with the proximity of key regional allies and a large forward deployed force allows the United States to amass military might sufficient to defeat or deter any North Korean aggression. Moreover, U.S. and allied military power is sufficient to compel Pyongyang to change its behavior. This force can be applied directly against North Korea or indirectly in the form of blockade or quarantine.

The United States also has the ability to control the information "high ground." Washington and its allies can collect and process intelligence on North Korea's political and military intentions at a level far superior to what Pyongyang can hope to achieve in return. The United States can also use its status as a global superpower to shape through public diplomacy the issues regarding North Korea. An information campaign outlining U.S. objectives can be directed at American, Japanese, and South Korean audiences in order to build support among the domestic populations. Similar information can be directed toward the North Korean citizenry in order to counter propaganda from Pyongyang.

Building a Comprehensive Strategy

The United States must politically re-engage North Korea. Washington's policy of shunning Pyongyang has not brought about desired changes and has arguably contributed to the increased nuclear and ballistic missile threat facing the United States and its allies. Furthermore, what little engagement Washington and its allies have had with Pyongyang has been uncoordinated and disjointed. Food aid is provided at the same time that economic sanctions are enforced. Washington includes Pyongyang in the "axis of evil" while it helps build nuclear reactors to ease the North's electric power concerns. Signals are mixed and it is difficult—nearly impossible—to explain U.S. policy at home and abroad.

The United States needs a comprehensive, coordinated, and integrated strategy for North Korea. This strategy must be clearly articulated and based on incentives for Pyongyang to change its behavior. Each North Korean move in a positive direction should be rewarded; negative actions should be punished. This carrot and stick policy must be applied evenly and multilaterally. If the United States, Japan, and South Korea can include China and Russia as partners in bringing about desired changes in North Korea, the likelihood of success is high.

To what standards should the United States hold North Korea? Fortunately, there are several established international agreements or regimes whereby North Korean compliance will help the United States reach its strategic objectives. The most important is the Agreed Framework between the United States and North Korea signed in 1994. Designed to freeze Pyongyang's fledgling nuclear program, the agreement calls for North Korea to halt development of nuclear weapons and shut down its graphite-moderated nuclear reactors that are capable of generating weapons-grade plutonium from spent fuel. In return, the United States, Japan, and South Korea would supply alternate energy in the form of heavy oil and construct a series of light-water reactors capable of supplying electric power, but less likely to provide weapons-grade material as a by-product.[12]

A key provision of the agreement is that North Korea must allow International Atomic Energy Agency (IAEA) inspectors to investigate all of its nuclear-capable facilities. Pyongyang has not done this, raising suspicions (later confirmed) that a parallel nuclear program is

---

[12] "Agreed Framework Between the United States of America and the Democratic People's Republic of Korea," U.S.-DPRK Agreed Framework, Carnegie Endowment for International Peace, 21 October 1994. <http://www.ceip.org/files/projects/npp/resources/koreaaf htm> (7 October 2002).

underway at secret locations or sites developed since the Agreed Framework was signed.[13] North Korea has countered this by stating that the framework only calls for IAEA compliance once "a significant portion of the [light-water reactor] project is completed, but before delivery of key nuclear components."[14] Since construction has only begun on the reactors, Pyongyang maintains that it is following the letter, if not the spirit, of the agreement.

The United States can alleviate this predicament by re-affirming the Agreed Framework and quickly supporting completion of the light-water reactors. Woefully behind schedule, construction on the plants should be expedited. Washington should claim that once the first light-water plant is built, but before fuel is provided, Pyongyang must allow IAEA inspectors access to all nuclear-related facilities. North Korea must again agree to halt work on its nuclear weapon program and include the new sites in the IAEA inspection regime.

Curtailing North Korean proliferation of ballistic missiles should focus on the Missile Technology Control Regime (MTCR) established in 1987. The MTCR seeks to prevent the transfer of ballistic and cruise missiles capable of delivering a 500-kilogram payload to a range of 300 kilometers.[15] To date, Pyongyang has refused to abide by the international norms of the MTCR. The United States should make acceptance of these standards the minimum requirement for North Korea. If accepted, the MTCR would prohibit Pyongyang from selling No Dong and Taepo Dong missiles and related technology to other states.

---

[13] Paul Kerr, "Undefined Strategy," The Washington Times, 1 September 2002, Commentary, p. B03. LexisNexis Academic (2 October 2002).

[14] Kerr, "Undefined Strategy."

[15] "How Effective is the MTCR?" Proliferation News and Resources, Carnegie Endowment for International Peace, 12 April 2001, <http://www.ceip.org/files/nonprolif/templates/PublicationID=672.htm> (7 October 2002).

In addition, the United States should demand that North Korea limit missile development to those with ranges less than 1,000 kilometers. Such Short-Range Ballistic Missiles (SRBMs) would be adequate for North Korea's defense, but would not pose a serious threat to Japan. Pyongyang has countered that its Taepo Dong program is designed to develop a commercial space launch capability—not a ballistic missile force. The United States, in concert with China and Russia, should offer to launch North Korean commercial payloads with domestic boosters, alleviating Pyongyang's need for long-range missiles.[16] North Korea is realizing that its missile program's greatest value lies as a bargaining chip.[17] Pyongyang, with assistance from Moscow, has framed the outlines of a unilateral ban on missile development, hoping to link this ban to U.S. concessions. The United States should embrace this framework as a starting point for missile negotiations.[18]

There are several "carrots" that the United States and its allies can offer North Korea for compliance with these accords. Initial support should focus on humanitarian assistance. The United States, South Korea, and Japan, must ensure that food aid is provided in sufficient quantities to eliminate the threat of starvation. Non-governmental organizations (NGOs) should monitor the delivery and distribution of the food to ensure it gets to where it is needed most. Using NGOs will also reduce North Korean fears that the United States or its allies will use this opportunity to infiltrate agents tasked with undermining the Pyongyang regime.

---

[16] Jon B. Wolfsthal, "North Korea: Hard Line is Not the Best Line," Policy Briefs and Economic Indicators, Columbia International Affairs Online, Carnegie Endowment for International Peace, June 2001, <http://www.ciaonet.org/pbei/ceip/woj07 html> (2 October 2002).

[17] Sean D. Murphy, "North Korean Nuclear Proliferation," The American Journal of International Law, October, 1999, v. 93-4, pp. 908-910. ProQuest. (2 October 2002).

[18] "What Is to Be Done With The Axis of Evil?" Proliferation News and Resources, Carnegie Endowment for International Peace, 6 February 2002, <http://www.ceip.org/files/nonprolif/templates/PublicationID=905 htm> (7 October 2002).

Economic benefits beyond humanitarian aid should be phased in as Pyongyang begins to accept the nuclear and missile proliferation measures mentioned above.[19] American, Japanese, and South Korean firms can increase trade with North Korea with an eye toward establishing joint-production or turnkey operations on terms favorable to Pyongyang. If the North continues to exhibit progress, the United States and its allies should consider establishing a Korean reconstruction fund within the World Bank or Asian Development Bank.[20] In each instance, the United States must clearly state that new incentives will be added in response to positive actions from Pyongyang.

The United States can also provide military incentives. First and foremost, Washington can offer to negotiate a final peace treaty to the Korean War—a key point for Pyongyang. This process should be linked to an agreement from both sides to reduce the size and forward deployment of their armed forces. If North Korea shows progress in reducing its military threat, the United States can offer a range of assurances ranging from a pledge of non-aggression to the suspension of joint military exercises with South Korea. Should this succeed, the United States can offer to begin a phased reduction of U.S. troops deployed to South Korea. In the initial phase, a portion of U.S. troops can be redeployed to Japan—out of South Korea, but close enough to threaten Pyongyang should it renege on pledges to reduce its own forces.

Diplomatically, the United States can offer North Korea something it perhaps cherishes most—international recognition. Washington should offer to normalize relations with

---

[19] Richard L. Armitage, "A Comprehensive Approach to North Korea." The Strategic Forum, Institute for National Strategic Studies, n. 159, March 1999, <http://www.ndu.edu/inss/strforum/forum159.html> (8 October 2002). Food/Economic Assistance/Sanctions.

[20] Armitage, Food/Economic Assistance/Sanctions.

Pyongyang, welcoming the North into the family of nations. This carrot should be offered last, as a "reward" for complete North Korean compliance with U.S. objectives.

What "sticks" can Washington employ should North Korea choose not to cooperate on these issues? Initially, the United States can simply withhold the incentives outlined above. This can be done cheaply and easily. As incentives were phased in according to North Korea compliance, they can be phased out in reverse order starting with diplomatic recognition and proceeding through military, economic, and aid programs. At each phase, the United States must clearly articulate that it is removing a carrot based on North Korean non-compliance.

If withholding incentives does not work, applying diplomatic or economic sanctions will escalate pressure on Pyongyang. The United States can seek to condemn North Korean behavior in the United Nations and affect the actions of others toward North Korea via Washington's influence in the World Bank or International Monetary Fund. Direct economic sanctions can be applied in certain circumstances, but the dictatorship of Kim Jong-Il and the decrepit nature of the North's economy make them ill-suited for broad-based applications.[21] Specific sanctions, for instance, can target North Korean attempts to deliver missiles or related technologies and involve the interdiction of ships carrying this materiel.

Militarily, the United States and its allies can work to strengthen its deterrent posture on the peninsula. This can initially be done in a non-threatening manner by underscoring the importance of the U.S.-Japan alliance.[22] Washington can also highlight Pyongyang's sense of isolation by making high-profile visits to allies in the region as well as China and Russia. The

---

[21] Chantal de Jonge Oudraat, "Making Economic Sanctions Work," Survival, v. 42, n. 3, Autumn 2000, p. 116.

[22] Armitage, Operational Elements of A New Comprehensive Approach.

United States can also ratchet up pressure on the North by reviewing the composition of U.S. forces in South Korea to ensure the proper mix of capabilities is present, increasing the number of troops deployed in the South, and increasing the frequency and intensity of joint exercises.

The ultimate stick is U.S. military intervention in North Korea. If Pyongyang continues to develop nuclear weapons and the missiles capable of delivering them against the United States, Washington and its allies should move to militarily erase this threat. This, of course, is the option of last resort. Relations with key allies and potential adversaries will be tested and, as Clausewitz so elegantly explained, chance, reason, and passion may interact to create unexpected outcomes.

Opportunities and Constraints

What are the benefits to be gained from a successful U.S. strategy against North Korea? Achieving a comprehensive peace agreement that includes the elimination of Pyongyang's nuclear weapon and long-range ballistic missile programs, along with a reduction in conventional military forces on both sides of the DMZ, will help normalize relations in North Asia and reduce tensions felt in Seoul, Pyongyang, Tokyo, and even Beijing.[23] Most of all, it will allow regional governments to free resources that were applied to defense and redirect them toward constructive pursuits—such as economic development in the region.

A reduced military threat from North Korea will permit the United States to withdraw forces from the peninsula. Since the end of the cold war, U.S. military commitments have grown to the point where nearly half a million American soldiers are stationed in over 146 countries.[24]

---

[23] Wolfsthal, "North Korea: Hard Line is Not the Best Line."

[24] "DoD 101, An Introductory Overview of the Department of Defense." Defense Link, U.S. Department of Defense, October, <www.dod mil/pubs/dod101> (13 October 2002).

This is a tremendous financial burden on the United States, particularly at a time when Washington is striving to transform its military into a lighter, more mobile force. American units assigned to Korea are considered "heavy" forces and are prepared to fight a conventional force-on-force war. The opportunity to disengage from this commitment without jeopardizing peace on the peninsula is a tremendous benefit for a military looking to reinvent itself.

The elimination of the long-range ballistic missile threat from North Korea will take some of the pressure off the United States to develop and deploy a National Missile Defense (NMD) system.[25] As currently conceived, NMD would not be able to defeat an attack consisting of hundreds of missiles. Its value lies in defeating the threat posed by rogue nations with limited arsenals. Of these countries, only North Korea is potentially capable of striking U.S. territory. If this threat is eliminated, the United States has more time to either reassess its need for NMD or develop a more effective system.

Successful engagement with North Korea can also pay dividends for U.S. relations with China and Russia. With a multilateral approach, the United States can include both countries in helping set the framework for negotiations with Pyongyang, thus making it clear that Beijing and Moscow will benefit from cooperation or share the burden of failure.[26] Washington can also approach China and Russia bilaterally, offering economic or diplomatic incentives for both countries to play a constructive role in North Korea. If either approach is successful, the U.S. alliance structure in North Asia will be strengthened.

While the benefits are many, there are also several constraints. A U.S. engagement strategy involving incremental incentives is necessarily a long-term approach. If North Korea is

---

[25] Wolfsthal, "North Korea: Hard Line is Not the Best Line."

[26] Armitage, Foundation for a New Approach.

committed to developing nuclear weapons and long-range missiles, it could use U.S. overtures to buy the time needed to complete these programs.[27] The United States is counting on the Agreed Framework to halt North Korean nuclear programs, but, as we have seen, this agreement is not sufficiently robust to deter Pyongyang from cheating.

Another constraint involves the possibility that regional powers will not embrace the U.S. strategy and pursue individual policies toward North Korea. Beijing, Moscow, Tokyo, and Seoul share common interests with the United States regarding North Korea, but they may not share our goals or our approach toward achieving them. China has resisted active cooperation with the Agreed Framework, with the World Food Program, and on eliminating the proliferation of missiles.[28] In pursuing its "sunshine policy," Seoul has taken steps toward the North that have sometimes been at odds with U.S. objectives. Without a multilateral approach, the United States would find it extremely difficult to achieve any kind of success with North Korea.

II.

The four U.S. objectives identified above can certainly be achieved via peaceful means. Despite setbacks, some diplomatic progress has been made toward eliminating North Korea's nuclear and long-range ballistic missile programs. Even South Korean President Kim Dae Jung's sunshine policy toward Pyongyang is establishing the necessary groundwork toward the possible reunification of the two countries. Nonetheless, part two of this paper assumes that the United States learns that North Korea is close to deploying nuclear weapons or has developed

---

[27] Armitage, Who Is Buying Time?

[28] Armitage, Foundation for a New Approach.

ballistic missiles capable of striking the United States. In this case, military intervention may be the best—and only—option for Washington and its allies.

Political Setting and Objectives

Washington has four political objectives going into a military conflict with North Korea. First and foremost, the United States must have the direct support of South Korea and Japan. These two nations are most affected by North Korean belligerence and their willingness to accept U.S. direction regarding the employment of troops, access to staging areas, and defense of critical lines of communication is a prerequisite for success in any conflict against the North.

Second, Washington will seek to ensure that China and Russia stay out of the conflict and not provide direct or indirect assistance to Pyongyang. Widening a peninsula war into a World War is the last thing the United States and its allies want. The best possible scenario in this regard is to ally Moscow and Beijing with the coalition prior to the start of hostilities. This would send a powerful message to Pyongyang highlighting the North's isolation.

Third, the United States wants to capture or destroy North Korea's nuclear weapons and ballistic missiles, eliminating this serious threat. If military intervention were the last resort, then Washington's fourth objective would be the total defeat of the North Korean military and the reunification of Korea under the democratic government in Seoul.

North Korea's political goals are completely opposite. Kim Jong-Il's primary objective is to remain in power. To ensure this, he will attempt to drive a wedge between the United States and its coalition allies, make overtures toward China and Russia in an effort to gain their alliance or neutrality, and work to ensure the survival of the North's military might—including its weapons of mass destruction.

Military Strategic Setting

Washington and its coalition partners have the military resources necessary to attain these objectives. This is predicated, of course, on the assumption that the United States is not already engaged in another major military conflict. Coalition operations against the North will encumber the bulk of U.S. strategic lift assets, not to mention strike aircraft and Special Operations Forces (SOF). These forces must be applied early in the conflict and cannot be tied up conducting missions elsewhere around the globe.

Although it is the most powerful nation in the world, the United States must prepare to fight a conventional war against the North. Since the impetus for military intervention is the removal of nuclear weapons from the peninsula, the United States cannot initiate the use of such weapons without rebuke. Washington, however, must warn Pyongyang that if the North employs nuclear, biological, or chemical weapons against coalition forces or allies, the United States is able to respond in kind with overwhelming force.

The United States will fight a coalition war. Washington expects South Korea to fight along side U.S. forces throughout the conflict. Japan is expected to allow U.S. forces to stage and strike from her territory as well as to defend coalition forces on the islands and along the sea lines of communication between Japan and the Korean Peninsula. Should China or Russia join the coalition against North Korea, their conventional military will add overwhelming force to the campaign.

North Korea will fight alone. Pyongyang can be expected to defend itself initially with conventional weapons—saving any nuclear, biological, or chemical weapons capability as a bargaining chip to stop hostilities or strike allies should they threaten the survival of the ruling regime.

Military Objectives

North Korea's center of gravity is its authoritarian regime. It is critical for the U.S.-led coalition to quickly sever Kim Jong-Il's ability to command and control his military forces. This is particularly important when confronting the threat of nuclear weapons and ballistic missiles—where authority for use is undoubtedly centralized at the top. Disrupting strategic command and control will also prohibit North Korean forces from quickly reacting to the superior mobility of U.S. forces.

In addition to "decapitating" the North Korean leadership, coalition forces would seek to locate, isolate, and destroy known nuclear weapon and ballistic missile sites before the North can relocate or use these weapons. Coalition forces would also seek to isolate North Korea's frontline forces by interdicting enemy lines of communication and supply. Once these units are cut off from reinforcement, coalition forces can move to destroy them. Defensively, coalition forces will strive to ensure that Seoul is not overrun and that Pusan and other key ports and airfields remain operational.

Pyongyang understands that the center of gravity for the U.S.-led coalition is its political unity. If the North can drive a wedge between the United States and South Korea or Japan, the coalition's ability to effectively carry on the fight will be destroyed. The best way for North Korea to achieve this objective is to rapidly increase the political cost of the war. This can be accomplished through escalation—by using weapons of mass destruction against coalition cities. It can also be gained through inflicting casualties on the battlefield at a rate beyond what public support in the coalition countries will tolerate. Kim Jong-Il realizes that if he can undermine U.S. public support for the war, his stands a good chance of surviving the conflict.

The war cannot end before all North Korean nuclear weapons are captured or destroyed, all long-range ballistic missiles (and related production facilities) are eliminated, the North Korean military is defeated, and the regime in Pyongyang removed from power. Any termination short of this is doomed to failure. Coalition forces will need to occupy North Korea to install a local government, rebuild key infrastructure, maintain order, and ensure that other nations, such as China and Russia, refrain from undermining U.S. efforts for the new, unified Korea.

Military Capabilities and Vulnerabilities

The U.S. military is the strongest and most capable in the world.[29] As shown in Operations DESERT STORM and ENDURING FREEDOM, the U.S. military is able to project power around the globe and apply it in unique ways. There is no doubt that the United States and its coalition partners have the military means to win a conventional conflict with North Korea. Coalition forces would command the skies and the seas, and present sufficient land power to defend the DMZ against the superior numbers of the North Korean Army. Although the North Korean military will initially outnumber coalition forces on the ground (about 1,000,000 to 600,000), the United States and its allies should be able to apply superior technology in weaponry and intelligence, as well as flexibility in battlefield command and control to defeat the North.[30]

Despite its high technology force, the United States has low technology vulnerabilities. First and foremost is the need to quickly augment the 37,000 U.S. troops stationed in South Korea. The United States must transport men and materiel in large numbers into South Korea

---

[29] U.S. Department of Defense, Quadrennial Defense Review Report, 30 September 2001 (Washington, D.C., 2001), 7-8.

[30] "2000 Report to Congress: Military Situation on the Korean Peninsula," Supporting the Allied War Effort.

and Japan. This effort will require tremendous airlift and sealift; but more importantly, will require secure debarkation points.[31] In addition to reinforcements, the United States faces the vulnerability of coalition warfare. Washington must coordinate its military operations with Seoul and Tokyo, which may not agree to strategic or tactical decisions regarding the war. As Clausewitz envisioned, this facet will undoubtedly add a source of friction to coalition forces not found with their North Korean opponents.[32]

Coalition forces will be facing the fifth largest military in the world.[33] North Korea's ground forces, numbering one million active duty soldiers, provide the bulk of their offensive warfighting capability and are the world's third largest army.[34] Seventy percent of their active forces, including 700,000 troops, 8,000 artillery pieces, and 2,000 tanks, are garrisoned within 100 miles of the DMZ—many protected by tunnels and other underground facilities.[35] The strength of the North Korean forces is their sheer numbers and ability to apply tremendous artillery fire across the DMZ as far south as Seoul. The North's asymmetric capability is also quite formidable. Pyongyang maintains an inventory of over 500 short-range SCUD ballistic missiles as well as undetermined quantities of medium-range No Dong and Taepo Dong ballistic

---

[31] "2000 Report to Congress: Military Situation on the Korean Peninsula," Supporting the Allied War Effort.

[32] Carl von Clausewitz, On War, ed. & trans. Michael Howard & Peter Paret (Princeton: Princeton University Press, 1976), 119.

[33] "2000 Report to Congress: Military Situation on the Korean Peninsula," Section Two: Democratic Peoples Republic of Korea (DPRK) Forces. Military Forces.

[34] "2000 Report to Congress: Military Situation on the Korean Peninsula," Section Two: Democratic Peoples Republic of Korea (DPRK) Forces. Military Forces.

[35] "2000 Report to Congress: Military Situation on the Korean Peninsula," Section Two: Democratic Peoples Republic of Korea (DPRK) Forces. Military Forces.

missiles.[36] These missiles can be armed with chemical and biological weapons and target coalition forces, cities, and debarkation points. North Korea's Special Operation Forces are also the largest in the world, consisting of over 100,000 elite troops that can act as a force multiplier against coalition forces.[37]

While North Korea presents a formidable opponent, they have vulnerabilities that can be exploited. First and foremost is Pyongyang's rigid command and control process. The North has prepared for a conventional conflict based on traditional force-on-force operations. The United States has demonstrated that it can apply its firepower and technology in unusual ways, forcing the enemy to react to U.S. initiatives. Tactical flexibility is not an advantage for the North and may lead to an uncoordinated response to coalition strikes. Combined arms operations are another vulnerability for Pyongyang. North Korean ground forces will dominate operations leaving command of the air and sea lines of communication to coalition forces. Finally, logistics have been a traditional vulnerability for the North. After the Korean War, Pyongyang decided to stockpile reserves of weapons and materiel.[38] Although these reserves are substantial, they must be transported and distributed to front-line forces, leaving them open to coalition air strikes.

Strategic Concept

---

[36] "2000 Report to Congress: Military Situation on the Korean Peninsula," Section Two: Democratic Peoples Republic of Korea (DPRK) Forces. Military Forces.

[37] U"2000 Report to Congress: Military Situation on the Korean Peninsula," Section Two: Democratic Peoples Republic of Korea (DPRK) Forces. Military Forces.

[38] U"2000 Report to Congress: Military Situation on the Korean Peninsula," Section Two: Democratic Peoples Republic of Korea (DPRK) Forces. Logistics and Sustainability.

The coalition strategy will emphasize the application of overwhelming technology, maneuver, and surprise. Coalition air forces will strike first to disrupt North Korea's command and control and air defense capability. Air power will be used concurrently to strike targets associated with Pyongyang's weapons of mass destruction program and logistical choke points and stockpiles. Finally, the full weight of the coalition air campaign will be applied toward the destruction of North Korea's ground forces.

Coalition ground forces will apply both a direct and indirect approach against the North. Heavy ground forces will defend the DMZ and conduct massive counter battery fire against North Korean artillery forces. Lighter, more mobile forces—including U.S. Marines—will conduct amphibious landings along both littorals and behind enemy lines. These forces will strive to capture the North's nuclear- and ballistic missile-associated facilities. It is imperative that these forces strike quickly before North Korean defenders can react.

Coalition naval forces will defend the vital sea lines of communication between the United States and Japan, and between Japan and the Korean Peninsula. Naval forces will also insert SOF forces prior to the start of hostilities, mine North Korean ports, support the amphibious landings, and conduct cruise missile and carrier air strikes against North Korean targets.

Prior to the start of hostilities and throughout the conflict, coalition SOF will penetrate enemy defenses, identify key North Korean targets, destroy high priority nuclear and ballistic missile facilities, and support coalition landings behind enemy lines.

The North Korean military strategy will probably stress limited objectives, such as the cessation of fighting and a return to the bargaining table.[39] This can best be accomplished by

---

[39] Robert Karnoil, "North Korea: Rational 'Rogue'," Jane's Defense Weekly, 10 July 2002, <http://www4.janes.com/content1/janesdata/mags/jdw/jdw01953 htm> (2 October 2002).

quickly raising the political and military costs of the war for the coalition. The North can strike hard with artillery and ground forces at Seoul and employ ballistic missiles against mobilization and debarkation sites in the South. If this fails, then Pyongyang is likely to expand the war by striking at coalition forces and cities in Japan. Kim Jong-Il will hope that eroding public support in the South, Japan, and even the United States will force a stop to the fighting. If coalition forces threaten the survival of the North Korean regime, Kim Jong-Il is likely to order the use of chemical or biological weapons first against the South and possibly against Japan.

Potential Results

North Korea is facing a war it cannot win. Pyongyang's conventional military might is diminishing relative to coalition forces, forcing the North to rely on weapons of mass destruction for deterrence and defense. It is precisely these weapons of mass destruction that are isolating Pyongyang from potential allies and building the international coalition forcing their removal.[40] If coalition forces strike North Korea and Pyongyang chooses not to use weapons of mass destruction, they will be defeated. If the North uses these weapons, it will have proved the international case against itself, forcing coalition forces to use whatever means necessary to disarm North Korea and remove Kim Jong-Il from power.

The political, economic, military, and humanitarian costs of war on the Korean Peninsula depend on the ability of coalition forces to destroy or neutralize North Korean weapons of mass destruction before they can be employed in the conflict. If this is achieved, coalition forces will win, but the cost in terms of military and civilian casualties will be substantial.[41] Should North

---

[40] "U.S. Tells N. Korea Disarm or Face Global Pressure."

[41] Trainor. "A Second Korean War?"

Korea unleash weapons of mass destruction upon the South and Japan, the coalition will ultimately win, but the costs would rise exponentially. Not only would military and civilian casualties skyrocket, but the political and economic costs in terms of public fear, eroded international standards of behavior, and destroyed industrial infrastructure, make the next Korean War something the world hasn't seen since 1945.

Conclusion

The standoff between Washington and Pyongyang is fraught with peril. The United States wants North Korea to eliminate the weapons Pyongyang believes are increasingly necessary for its own survival. Domestically, North Korea is facing starvation and economic ruin. Internationally, Pyongyang is isolated and increasingly viewed as a pariah by former allies. The North's only means for survival rests with those nations allied against it. A rational North Korea would seek to accommodate the United States through diplomatic bargaining, trading its weapons of mass destruction for the means to rescue its people and preserve its leadership.

But Kim Jong-Il does not always act rationally. The North may only be interested in buying time until it can field these weapons and extort the support it needs to survive. If this is the case, coalition forces have the conventional capability to defeat North Korea, eliminate its weapons of mass destruction, and replace the ruling regime. While the future for Pyongyang is bleak, how much is the United States willing to pay to achieve its objectives? The stakes are too high to continue a policy of isolation. U.S. engagement, employing a multilateral approach where incentives and sanctions are linked to North Korean behavior, is the best answer.

BIBLIOGRAPHY

"2000 Report to Congress: Military Situation on the Korean Peninsula." Defense Link. U.S. Department of Defense. September 2000. <http://www.defenselink.mil/news/Sep2000/korea0912000.html> (19 October 2002).

Albright, David, Holly Higgins, and Kevin O'Neill. "Solving the North Korean Nuclear Puzzle." Institute for Strategic International Studies. 2002. <http://www.isisonline.org/publications/dprk/book/epilogue.html> (8 October 2002).

"Agreed Framework Between the United States of America and the Democratic People's Republic of Korea." U.S.-DPRK Agreed Framework. Carnegie Endowment for International Peace. 21 October 1994. <http://www.ceip.org/files/projects/npp/resources/koreaaf.htm> (7 October 2002).

Armitage, Richard L. "A Comprehensive Approach to North Korea." The Strategic Forum. Institute for National Strategic Studies. n. 159. March 1999. <http://www.ndu.edu/inss/strforum/forum159.html> (8 October 2002).

"Asia: Strange Meeting; North Korea and America." The Economist. 3 August 2002. v. 364. p.51. ProQuest (2 October 2002).

Bandow, Doug. "Hugs for Pyongyang." The Washington Times. 4 October 1999. Cato Institute. <http://www.cato.org/cgi-bin/scripts/printtech.cgi/dailys/10-08-99.html> (8 October 2002).

Bandow, Doug. "Rethinking the North Korea Threat." Newsday. 22 August 2002. Cato Institute. <http://www.cato.org/cgi-bin/scripts/printtech.cgi/dailys/08-27-99.html> (8 October 2002).

Barilleaux, Ryan J. and Andrew Ilsu Kim. "Clinton, Korea, and Presidential Diplomacy." World Affairs. Summer 1999. v. 162-1. pp. 29-40. ProQuest (2 October 2002).

Clausewitz, Carl von. On War. Edited and Translated by Michael Howard and Peter Paret. Princeton: Princeton University Press, 1976.

"DoD 101, An Introductory Overview of the Department of Defense." Defense Link. U.S. Department of Defense. October. <http://www.dod.mil/pubs/dod101.html> (13 October 2002).

Eichensehr, Kristen. "Broken Promises." Harvard International Review. Fall 2001. v. 23-3. pp. 11-12. ProQuest (2 October 2002).

Gilinsky, Victor and Henry Sokolski. "These N. Korean Reactors Light Up Danger Signals." The Washington Post. 4 August 2002. Outlook. P. B02. LexisNexis Academic (2 October 2002).

Hoi-Chang, Lee. "Korea at the Crossroads: The Challenges Ahead." Heritage Lectures. The Heritage Foundation. No. 728. 23 January 2002. <http://www.heritage.org/library/lecture/hl728.html> (7 October 2002).

"How Effective is the MTCR?" Proliferation News and Resources. Carnegie Endowment for International Peace. 12 April 2001. <http://www.ceip.org/files/nonprolif/templates/PublicationID=672.htm> (7 October 2002).

Hwang, Balbina. "Overcoming The Stalemate on the Korean Peninsula." Heritage Lectures. The Heritage Foundation. n. 750. 8 May 2002. <http://www.heritage.org/hl750.htm> (7 October 2002).

Karnoil, Robert. "North Korea: Rational 'Rogue'," Jane's Defense Weekly. 10 July 2002. <http://www4.janes.com/content1/janesdata/jdw/jdw01953.htm> (2 October 2002).

Kerr, Paul. "Undefined Strategy." The Washington Times. 1 September 2002. Commentary. p. B03. LexisNexis Academic (2 October 2002).

Kimball, Daryl G. "Name-Calling or Nonproliferation?" Arms Control Today. March 2002. v. 32-2. p.2. ProQuest (2 October 2002).

"Korea, North." World Countries. Infoplease.com. 2002. <http://www.infoplease.com/ipa/A0107686.html> (2 October 2002).

Murphy, Sean D. "North Korean Nuclear Proliferation." The American Journal of International Law. October 1999. v. 93-4. pp. 908-910. ProQuest (2 October 2002).

"NBC Capabilities, Korea, North." Jane's Nuclear, Biological and Chemical Defense. 29 July 2002. <http://www4.janes.com/content1/janesdata.htm> (2 October 2002).

"North Korea: Armed Forces Structure." Periscope. June 2002. <http://www.periscope.ucg.com/docs/nations/asia/northkor/organzn/index.html> (2 October 2002).

Oudraat, Chantal de Jonge. "Making Economic Sanctions Work." Survival. v. 42. n. 3. Autumn 2000. pp. 105-27.

Pena, Charles V. "Axis of Evil: Tilting at Windmills." Cato Institute. 22 February 2002. <http://www.cato.org/cgi-bin/scripts/printtech.cgi/dailys/02-22-02.html> (8 October 2002).

Plunk, Daryl M. "Time For A New North Korea Policy." Backgrounder. The Heritage Foundation. 2 July 1999. n. 1304. <http://www.heritage.org/bg1304.htm> (8 October 2002).

"Special Report: Know Thine Enemy—Weapons Proliferation." The Economist. 2 February 2002. v. 362. pp. 24-26. ProQuest (2 October 2002).

Tenet, George J. "Dangers and Threats to the U.S.: Countries That Could Cause Problems." <u>Vital Speeches of the Day</u>. 1 March 1999. v. 65-10. pp. 293-299. ProQuest (2 October 2002).

<u>The World Almanac and Book of Facts 2002</u>. New York: World Almanac Books, 2002.

Trainor, Bernard E. "A Second Korean War?" <u>Marine Corps Gazette</u>. August 1997. v. 81-8. pp. 26-7. ProQuest (2 October 2002).

Trulock, Notra. "Going Nuclear in North Korea; Regime May Have One or Two Bombs Already." The Washington Times. 25 June 2002. OPED. P. A19. LexisNexis Academic (2 October 2002).

U.S. Department of Defense. <u>Quadrennial Defense Review Report, 30 September 2001</u>. Washington, D.C., 2001.

"U.S. Tells N. Korea Disarm or Face Global Pressure." <u>World</u>. <u>CNN.com</u>. 19 October 2002. <http://www.cnn.com/2002/WORLD/asiapcf/east/10/19/nkorea.nukes/index.html> (19 October 2002).

Wagner, Alex. "Chronology of U.S.-North Korean Nuclear and Missile Diplomacy." <u>Fact Sheets</u>. Arms Control Association. April 2002. <http://www.armscontrol.org/factsheets/dprkchron.asp.html> (7 October 2002).

Wagner, Alex. "U.S. Missile Sanctions." <u>Fact Sheets</u>. Arms Control Association. March 2002. <http://www.armscontrol.org/factsheets/missanc.asp.html> (7 October 2002).

Weiss, Kenneth G. "The Limits of Diplomacy: Missile Proliferation, Diplomacy, and Defense." <u>World Affairs</u>. Winter 2001. v. 163-3. pp. 110-122. ProQuest (2 October 2002).

"What Is to Be Done With The Axis of Evil?" <u>Proliferation News and Resources</u>. Carnegie Endowment for International Peace. 6 February 2002. <http://www.ceip.org/files/nonprolif/templates/PublicationID=905.htm> (7 October 2002).

Wolfsthal, Jon B. "North Korea: Hard Line is Not the Best Line." <u>Policy Briefs and Economic Indicators</u>. <u>Columbia International Affairs Online</u>. Carnegie Endowment for International Peace. June 2001. <http://www.ciaonet.org/pbei/ceip/woj07.html> (2 October 2002).

Wortzel, Dr. Larry M. "North Korea: Too Much, Too Soon." <u>Press Room Commentary</u>. The Heritage Foundation. 25 October 2000. <http://www.heritage.org/Press/Commentary/ed102500.htm> (8 October 2002).

Wright, David. "Cut North Korea Some Slack." <u>Bulletin of the Atomic Scientists</u>. March/April 1999. v. 55. n. 2. <http://www.bullatomsci.org/issues/1999/ma99/ma99wright.html> (2 October 2002).